ANIMALS *in* DANGER

Bengal Tiger

Rod Theodorou

Heinemann Library
Chicago, Illinois

Designed by Ron Kamen
Illustrations by Dewi Morris/Robert Sydenham
Originated by Ambassador Litho
Printed by South China Printing in Hong Kong / China

05 04 03 02 01
10 9 8 7 6 5 4 3 2 1

Library of Congress Cataloging-in-Publication Data
Theodorou, Rod.
     Bengal Tiger / Rod Theodorou.
              p. cm. – (Animals in danger)
       Includes bibliographical references (p.).
       Summary: Describes the habitat, behavior, and endangered status of Bengal tigers and suggests ways to help save them from extinction.
       ISBN 1-57572-267-4 (library)
       1. Tigers—Juvenile literature. 2. Endangered species—Juvenile literature. [1. Tigers.
       2. Endangered species.] I. Title.

QL737.C23 T4733 2000
599.756—dc21
                                                                00-026791

Acknowledgments
The author and publishers are grateful to the following for permission to reproduce copyright material: FLPA/ Fritz Polking, p. 4, FLPA/ Eichhorn Zingel, p. 4, FLPA/ Jurgen & Christine Sohns, pp. 5, Gerard Lacz pp.6, 15, FLPA/ M. Newman p. 7, FLPA/ Terry Whittaker p. 16, FLPA/ E. & D. Hosking p. 21, FLPA/ John Holmes p. 25; NHPA/ Martin Harvey, p. 26; Oxford Scientific Films, p. 8, Oxford Scientific Films/ Daniel J. Cox, p. 4, Oxford Scientific Films/ Miriam Austerman, p. 9, Oxford Scientific Films/ Belinda Wright, pp. 11, 17, 19, 22, 24, Oxford Scientific Films/ Mahipal Singh, p. 12, Oxford Scientific Films/ Mike Birkhead, p. 13, Oxford Scientific Films/ Alfred B. Thomas, p. 14, Oxford Scientific Films/ Zig Leszczynski, p. 18, Oxford Scientific Films/ Tim David, p. 20; Still Pictures/ Roland Seitre, p. 23, Still Pictures/ Valmik Thapar, p. 27.

Cover photograph reproduced with permission of Bruce Coleman.
Special thanks to Henning Dräger for his comments in the preparation of this book.

Every effort has been made to contact copyright holders of any material reproduced in this book. Any omissions will be rectified in subsequent printings if notice is given to the publisher.

Some words are shown in bold, **like this.** You can find out what they mean by looking in the glossary.

Contents

Animals in Danger

black rhino

Florida manatee

giant panda

All over the world, more than 10,000 animal species are in danger. Some are in danger because their homes are being destroyed. Many are in danger from people hunting them.

This book is about Royal Bengal tigers and why they are **endangered**. Unless people **protect** them, Bengal tigers will become **extinct**. We will only be able to find out about them from books.

What Is a Tiger?

Tigers are large **mammals**. They are the largest of the cat family. There is only one **species** of tiger, but there are five subspecies, or types.

The five types are the Siberian tiger, the South China tiger, the Indochinese tiger, the Royal Bengal tiger and the Sumatran tiger. Three other types have become **extinct** in the last 70 years.

What Do Bengal Tigers Look Like?

Bengal tigers have a striped coat. It is hard to see them in the shadows of the forest. This helps them to hide from their **prey** and from hunters.

Most Bengal tigers have orange, brown, black and white stripes. Some tigers have very light colored fur. These are called white tigers. They are very rare.

Where Do Bengal Tigers Live?

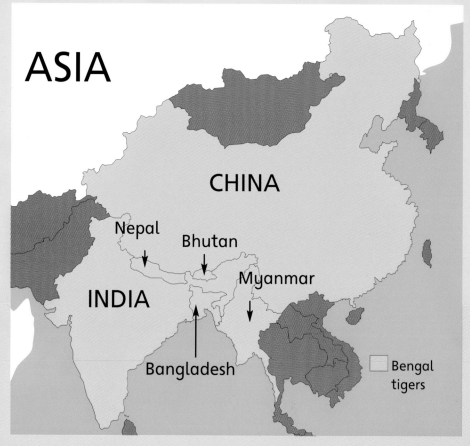

Bengal tigers live across the **continent** of Asia.
They live in hot countries where there are long
grasses and thick forests full of animals to hunt.

10

Bengal tigers do not like too much heat. They spend their days resting in their **dens** or under trees. They come out at night when it is cool and dark. Then they can surprise their **prey**.

Bengal tigers are **carnivores**. They will eat most animals. They like large **mammals** best. They eat deer and wild pigs. Bengal tigers also eat small mammals, birds, frogs, and fish.

12

Bengal tigers hunt mostly early in the morning or in the evening. Their stripes help to hide them in the shadows of tall grasses. One big meal like a deer will fill a tiger for a few days.

Bengal tigers like to live and hunt alone. But the **males** and **females** meet in the spring to **mate.** The male leaves after they have mated. He does not help care for the babies.

About three months after mating, the female will give birth to three or four babies. They are called **cubs.** She will look after them in a **den** made from plants, in a cave, or in a rocky area.

Caring for the Cubs

Bengal tiger **cubs** are born blind and helpless like kittens. They drink their mother's milk for three to five months. Then she starts to teach them how to find food.

The cubs do not hunt alone until they are more than a year old. The mother needs to **protect** them from adult male tigers, who sometimes kill cubs.

Unusual Bengal Tiger Facts

Unlike most cats, Bengal tigers like water and are strong swimmers. Sometimes they hunt for fish and frogs in the water. Sometimes they rest in the water to keep cool.

18

The stripes on a tiger's coat are like human fingerprints. No two tigers ever have exactly the same pattern of stripes.

How Many Bengal Tigers Are There?

One hundred years ago there were about 60,000 Bengal tigers living in the wild. Now there may be as few as 4,500 left.

Nowadays, most Bengal tigers live in India. Very few tigers stilll live in the wild. Most live in special protected areas called **reserves**. In China there may only be about 30 Bengal tigers left.

Why IS the Bengal Tiger in Danger?

Bengal tigers are in danger because humans hunt and kill them. The hunters make money by selling the tiger skins and bones.

22

Tiger bones are used in some kinds of medicines believed to cure aches and pains. Tiger skins and teeth are made into expensive clothes, jewelry, and decorations like rugs.

The Bengal tigers' habitat is also being destroyed. Tigers need to live in thick forests or tall grasslands. But the forests are being cut down to make room for farming.

Sometimes the grasslands are cut down to make room for factories or to build houses for people. Without the forests and grasslands there are no animals for the tigers to hunt for food.

How is the Bengal Tiger Being Helped?

Bengal tigers are now protected by **law**. **Conservation** groups like the World Wildlife Fund (WWF) work to stop the hunting of tigers. They try to stop the selling of tiger skins and bones.

Conservation groups also work with governments to make new tiger **reserves**. Tigers can live in these reserves, safe from hunters. If they are not hunted, tiger numbers might begin to rise again.

Bengal Tiger Fact File

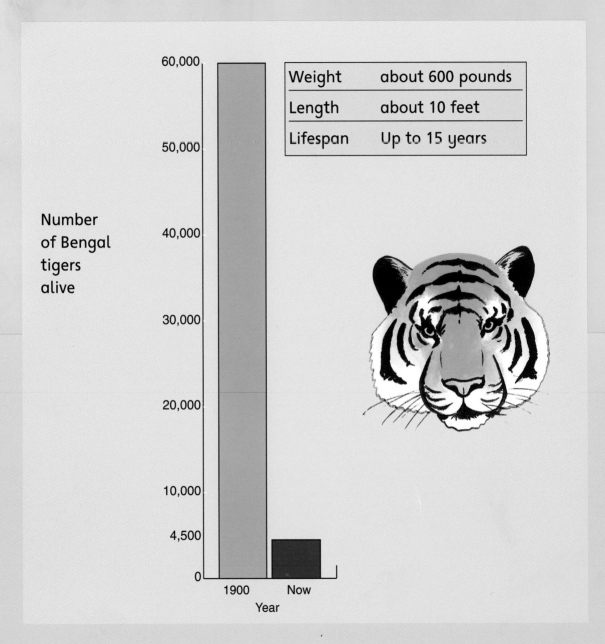

Number of Bengal tigers alive

Weight	about 600 pounds
Length	about 10 feet
Lifespan	Up to 15 years

Year

World Danger Table

	Number that may have been alive 100 years ago	Number that may be alive today
Giant panda	65,000	650
Blue whale	335,000	4,500
Black rhino	1,000,000	2,000
Mountain gorilla	85,000	500
Florida manatee	75,000	2,000

There are thousands of other animals in the world that are in danger of becoming **extinct**. This table shows some of these animals.

How Can You Help the Bengal Tiger?

If you and your friends raise money for the Bengal tigers, you can send it to these organizations. They take the money and use it to pay conservation workers, and to buy food and tools to help save the Bengal tiger.

Defenders of Wildlife
1101 Fourteenth Street, N.W. #1400
Washington, DC 20005

World Wildlife Fund
1250 Twenty-fourth Street
P.O. Box 97180
Washington, DC 20037

More Books to Read

Barron's Educational Staff. *Tiger.* Hauppage, N.J.: Barron's Educational Series, 2000.

Fichter, George S. *Endangered Animals.* New York: Golden Books Publishing Company, 1995.

Welsbacher, Anne. *Tigers.* Minneapolis, Minn.: ABDO Publishing Company, 2000.

30

Glossary

carnivore	animal that eats only meat
coat	hair that covers an animal's body
conservation	looking after things, especially if they are in danger
continent	large area of land, unbroken by sea, that can include many countries
den	place where wild animals live or hide
extinct	group of animals that has completely died out and can never live again
female	girl or woman
habitat	home or place where something lives
law	rule or something you have to do
male	boy or man
mammal	warm-blooded animals, like humans, that feed their young on their mother's milk
mate	when a male animal and a female animal come together to make baby animals
prey	animals that are hunted and killed by other animals
protected	kept safe
reserve	park or large area with guards that look after the animals
species	group of living things that are very similar

Index